Mud Pies
and
Jump Ropes

Deborah Hobbs Maloney

author

2015   Olmstead Publishing LLC

Mud Pies and Jump Ropes

Deborah Hobbs Maloney, author

Copyright 07 2015

Olmstead Publishing LLC

Art, Layout, Editing Dr Phyllis M Olmstead

Copyediting Chris Hammett

ISBN 978-1-934194-88-1

Olmstead Publishing LLC

OlmsteadPublishing@USA.com

www.Facebook.com/OlmsteadPublishing

www.OlmsteadPublishing.com

www.SquareUp.com/Market/Olmstead-Publishing-LLC

Dedication

I dedicate this book to my mom, my dad, my siblings, and my husband and daughter for the encouragement to continue to live my life to the fullest, even through all the grief and hard times. I realize I put all of you through a great deal for 46 years. However, your dedication to me when I was at my worst meant the world to me.

I also want to dedicate this book to John A. Dilullo, Jr., M.D. of neurology, the doctor who sent me to the physicians that finally were able to help me.

To neurologist and epileptologist Selim R. Benbadis, M.D. and neurosurgeon Fernando L. Vale, M.D. who operated on me.

To all the nurses and staff who cared for me at Tampa General Hospital, I thank you from the bottom of my heart.

Although I had much unrest with God during most of my life, He brought me through it by making me a strong willed person with the intentions to persevere and overcome this great affliction that I have had to deal with all my life. My life has truly turned out to be the miracle for which I have awaited.

Table of Contents

Introduction

How would you like to go through life living as though you were walking around in a stupor? Well, you wouldn't! I didn't enjoy it either, so I've chosen to write my life story to hopefully inspire and encourage others. I want parents of children that are having seizures and anyone else in this situation to realize that life isn't all peaches and cream.

Sometimes we have to endure a little bit of hell before we can get to heaven.

I have never quite figured out why God chose "me" to endure such a horrific life, but whatever His reason, I have lived a life full of seizures, doctor visits, medications, needles, electroencephalograms (EEGs) with sleep and sleep deprived, activity restrictions, and limited education since the age of nine and a half.

No one will ever know what it is like unless they have walked a day in my shoes. I would have loved to have participated in gymnastics or a dance class but, of course, that was out of the question. In the beginning, I was an active child and enjoyed playing outside. However, once I had my first grand mal seizure, I wasn't able to participate in physical education at school and my play time at home suffered greatly. I began to resent other children for being able to do what I couldn't. As time went on we found other things of interest that I was *able* to do, such as making mud pies in our carport, playing school, and jumping rope.

6

Chapter 1   Family Life

I was born in Geneva, Ohio, in the fall of 1958. I attended a small preschool and kindergarten in Middlefield, Ohio. The milkman would deliver our milk in little bottles each day for snack time at school. Along with the milk, we enjoyed graham crackers.

1. My Middlefield, Ohio Pre-K Class
Deborah—Third Row Down, Third Child from Left

There were many Amish people in the town of Middlefield and learning their culture was very interesting as a child. The sound of horse hooves on the road at all hours of the day and night was worth a look. The most amazing thing to watch was a barn-raising. All the Amish men and boys worked together and got the job done. The Amish men were excellent carpenters and the Amish women were great cooks. As a child I always admired their clothes. The boys and men all wore suspenders and black ties while the girls and women wore long dresses and bonnets. They all looked alike and there weren't any worries of who had the prettiest or newest clothes, cars, or homes.

On Sundays, the Amish families took turns having church in their barns. An Amish man, Norm Bender, helped my parents build their home in Middlefield. Because my dad worked for and managed the A&P Grocery Store in Middlefield, he was able to help Norm's daughter get a job at the store. She had to get permission to work at the A&P Store because she had to wear her Amish outfit to work. She worked for my dad for six years.

My dad expressed that he would like a store of his own someday. My grandfather, Albert Burgstaller, was planning to move to Florida so he said he would look for one once he settled. After Grandpa Burgstaller found a store in Ocala, Mom and Dad flew down to see it. The store was well maintained and in a good location. However, after getting back to Ohio, the real estate agent told Mom and Dad about another store near Lakeland that was only about five months old. Dad decided to return to Florida and ended up leasing the store and equipment in Gibsonia. After two years, and with my grandfather's backing, Dad purchased the store outright. My father's dream, at last, came true.

In May of 1965, my family moved to Florida. Inventory at the store took place on the 9th of May and on the 10^{th,} Mom and Dad took ownership. Dad took an idea from when he worked in Middlefield and put it into action. He gave 1% of the total amount of register receipts from the store to the local Boy Scout Troops and churches plus, he gave more than $13,000 to Padgett Elementary School.

Located in central Florida, Gibsonia was a very rural community. In fact, my dad's store was "the" store in town. Since then, central Florida has really grown, thanks in large part, to the development of popular tourist attractions/theme parks such as Disney World and Busch Gardens in the neighboring cities of Orlando and Tampa, respectively.

The grocery business lasted almost 19 years and then, because the big grocery chains came to our little town of Gibsonia, my dad was forced to make a decision about the store. After Thanksgiving 1983, Mom and Dad closed the grocery business. Dad ended up keeping one half of the store for a meat market and renting the other half for a bakery. That lasted a short while until Dad closed up shop completely.

In April of 1966, Gibsonia was hit hard by a tornado. I was in first grade at the time. Thank goodness the school only received minimal damage and we were all safe. However, going home was a different story for numerous children because many homes and businesses were badly damaged or completely gone. I remember that Dad left the store and ran as far as he could. His short trip was disrupted due to the debris and animals in the trees and on the roads. When he finally made it home, he and Mom came to pick me up at school.

I come from "a typical 1950s -1960s family" of a mother, father, and four children. Of two girls and two boys, I was eldest. I had been an only child for my first nine years. My parents wanted more children but Mom had struggled over the years with a number of miscarriages. In fact, my mother lost a baby before me and almost lost me. Dad had to carry her up and down the stairs at her mother and father's house because she was not allowed to climb stairs. Near the end of her pregnancy with me, she was put on complete bed rest. After having me, they tried again, but once more Mom miscarried the baby.

After moving to Florida, my parents spoke with Catholic Charities in 1968 regarding adoption. Much to their amazement, they received a phone call about three weeks later and Catholic Charities had a baby boy for them. They went to see him and lo and behold they came home with my new baby brother, Tim. At the time, Mom and Dad didn't realize it, but Tim was quite ill. The next morning Mom took Tim to our pediatrician, Dr. Henry Jefferson Redd, Jr. Dr. Redd was very insistent about them putting a vaporizer next to his crib and using a sheet to make a tent. Fortunately, after that rocky start, Tim's health improved.

Finally, at the age of nine, I had a sibling. I quickly learned how to change diapers and give bottles. Gee, what fun! Since my mom was needed to help out in the grocery store, my brother Tim was pretty much raised in the back room of the store where my parents had set up a playpen and high chair. When Tim was older, he, too, worked in the store. He especially liked working in the meat department.

Two and a half years later, my mother unexpectedly became pregnant and I became a sister to another brother, David. Eleven months after that "surprise," my mom had a baby girl, Diana. Where did they come from? After already having changed diapers, feeding, and bathing one brother, the next two, were a breeze. Again, I got to play mommy. It was great being the big sister. especially as time went on. Needless to say, I did a lot of babysitting for my mom. It was like having two families because of the age difference between Tim and me.

My parents have now been married for 58 years and both are still going strong. We were a middle-class, Catholic family who attended church regularly, sometimes with opposition from us kids. However, my parents believed that the family who prayed together, stayed together. Since we owned the grocery store, our family knew a lot of local people. In fact, Gibsonia was a tight-knit neighborhood where everyone knew each other. My friends and I attended the newly built Padgett Elementary School, located within walking distance of our home. Throughout our early years at Padgett, my mom would get up early and walk a group of neighborhood children, myself included, to the school. In the afternoon, Mom would be there waiting to walk all of us back home safely. She was met one day by a law enforcement officer who presented her with an award for walking us to and from school every day. This was a total surprise for her!

After school each day we could be found outside riding our bikes, roller skating up and down the street, sitting in the carport making mud pies, or scooping up tadpoles at the end of the driveway. Many days, my girlfriends and I would get together and play school. In the Girl Scouts of America, I started as a Brownie and continued all the way through to the Cadets. I took piano lessons for many years from an elderly lady, Mrs. Keckley, who lived just behind our grocery store. On piano lesson days, I would finish and walk up to our store for work or mom would come and get me. Along with having typical childhood fun, I enjoyed working in our grocery store with my dad. I would price the items on stock day and put them on the shelves, remembering to rotate the cans, boxes, or bagged items.

2. Piano Recital with Mrs. Keckley

My dad taught me a great deal about the grocery business and eventually I did much more than price items and stock shelves. I worked in the meat department wrapping meat for the meat case or vegetables for the produce case. My dad even tried to teach me how to cut up a chicken. That didn't go so well. We decided wrapping meats and produce were best suited for me.

On slow days and during the summer, Fleda Wood, my dad's right hand in the store, would allow me to run the cash register while she supervised. In those days, everything had to be rung up by hand as scanners hadn't yet been invented. Along with ringing up groceries, I quickly learned how to count change back to the customers, as we didn't have computerized registers that told us how much change to give until later years. At first, the new computerized registers were more of a hassle to learn than the old fashioned ones. However, once we got the hang of it, the computerized registers made things go more quickly. Still, everything had to be rung up by hand.

Besides owning the store and working together, our family took many fun vacations when we were young. Our best vacations were camping in the mountains. Tim was such an amazing Boy Scout, always teaching us about the plants and wildlife we encountered. We also spent many a weekend over at Daytona Beach during the summer. Playing in the sand and riding the waves was so awesome and refreshing from the hot Florida sun.

Things were good when I was little, but later, after the first seizure, I had to be watched like a hawk. Knee-deep water was all I could play in. Occasionally, I would sneak out a little further so I could ride in a wave.

Chapter 2 ∞   The Nightmare

In the spring of 1968, a few short months after Tim joined our family, I somehow contracted the Hong Kong Flu. For over a week, I was quite sick, in a weakened state, with a high fever that bounced back and forth between 101° and 106°. The doctor gave me a prescription, which I took during that week. By mid-week, I wasn't getting any better and shortly thereafter, my nightmare officially began.

I felt sick to my stomach and went to my mother's bedside to wake her. She said to me, "Maybe you are hungry, so let's go get something to eat."

Sitting at the table eating a bowl of Frosted Flakes™ cereal, I started to feel and act strange. I began to stare off into space and then my eyes began to roll back into my head. I was entering my first grand mal convulsion.

Not knowing what was happening my mother hysterically grabbed the phone, dialing 0 for the operator, as there was no 911 then. She ordered the operator to get the doctor. She felt extremely helpless and totally beside herself as she watched me convulsing on the floor. She passed the telephone to my dad who spoke to the doctor. The doctor insisted, "Put her in the car and go straight to the hospital. Don't wait for an ambulance!" Time was of the essence!

With Tim, just a tiny one at home, Mom ran to our neighbors and banged on the door. Mom yelled for our neighbor to get my brother as she was getting into the car. Our neighbor stayed with Tim for the rest of the night and into the following morning until other arrangements could be made.

We rushed to the hospital where the nightmare continued. Totally unresponsive in the Emergency Room, I turned a bluish-black color, so the doctors placed me in an oxygen tent and gave me medication to try to stop the convulsions.

Dr. Heath, who treated me in the ER, was also one of my pediatricians from The Children's Clinic. He became so exasperated and upset from working on me and trying desperately to get a response that he started trembling terribly. Due to his agitated state, he wasn't thinking clearly. He started to light up a cigarette. Another doctor, Dr. Moore, also a pediatrician from the The Children's Clinic, noticed that Dr. Heath was standing right next to my oxygen tent and rushed over to stop him before he could get the lighter to ignite.

Throughout my entire ordeal, my dad kept vigilant watch and informed my mom as things progressed. My mom was far too upset to come in the room where the doctors were working on me. Once the convulsing stopped and I came out of the seizure, the doctors placed me in the Intensive Care Unit (ICU) for three days followed by another seven days in a semi-private room. The nurses were instructed to strap my arms to the bed so I couldn't get out and hurt myself or pull out any of the IVs. The doctors placed me on the anti-seizure medications, Dilantin® and phenobarbital, fearing another seizure.

Back in those days, epilepsy was rather misunderstood by both science and religion. The Catholic Church considered it a sign or a curse and the only cure was an exorcism. Although an exorcism was never attempted on me, we did go to many novena prayer masses with hopes that God would choose to cure me. When a novena was held at the church, our family planned on attending for as many nights as we could. Novenas lasted for a total of nine nights, one hour a night. A Novena Mass was a prayer mass for anyone needing prayers over them for any reason. One could go forward and the priest would anoint them and say a prayer over them. This is why I became so upset with God when nothing ever changed for me. I continually had petit mal seizures and, later, more grand mals. Our family became particularly close with one priest, Father Renaldo. He even came for pizza at our house after the novena mass once or twice. He always carried Blessed Mother medals and gave them out to anyone who wanted one along with small Novena Prayer booklets.

At that time, children with seizures were often placed in hospitals and pushed aside because they weren't considered normal. Because of this, my parents wanted to keep my illness as quiet as possible. That was almost impossible due to our standing in the small community. As time passed people heard about my grand mal history. They asked the same question my parents and I kept asking, "What caused it?"

There were numerous possibilities. The high fever I had during my bout with the Hong Kong Flu or the drug they gave me to treat it could have triggered the first seizure. A head trauma or high fevers can cause many brain issues. We later learned that the drug I took for the flu had been known to cause convulsions in children. Or, was the cause something that happened earlier in my life?

When I was about 6 months old, I got mad as my dad was putting a sweatshirt on me. As he pulled it over my head, I flung myself backward hitting a high sharp baseboard in our house. The pediatrician told my mom to put ice on it and to try to keep me awake in case I had a concussion. Another time, at Brownie camp in 1968, I fell and hit my head. My parents felt that injury was the possible stimulus because it was just after that when I had the first grand mal seizure. There were so many factors that could have caused it. We didn't know which one to blame it on and the doctors were just as baffled. One thing was certain, my life changed completely that day in 1968. Much of the typical childhood activities I was used to became dangerous for me.

As I entered my pre-teen years, I began to realize the full effect of what I was experiencing on a daily basis. Although I had been on medication for over two years since the grand mal in the spring of 1968, it didn't help with the petit mal seizures. They came frequently and whenever they chose. I never knew when a seizure might begin or how bad it might become. No improvement happened for two years.

At the age of 15, mom and dad started letting me babysit to earn extra money. Along with babysitting my own brothers and sister, I landed a job babysitting two little boys one night a week while their parents bowled. Since I couldn't drive yet, they picked me up and took me home. Despite the petit mal seizures, I managed to live a semi-normal life.

When I turned 16, we weren't sure how to handle driving because of my seizures. Since the doctors never really diagnosed epilepsy, we were advised that I could get a driver's license and not say anything about the petit mals. I truly believe that doctors didn't believe that I was having the seizures, or didn't know what I was experiencing.

Once I began driving, I loved taking my brothers and sister to Disney World for the day. We would do this about once a month, just the four of us. I enjoyed taking them as much as they enjoyed going. We always made a long day of it. We would arrive when the park opened and stayed until we were ready to drop.

Chapter 3 ❧ A Childhood Taken Away

My childhood definitely became rather depressing. Heck, I had been through much by the age of ten, but there was so much more ahead of me. More than anyone could ever imagine…

I was restricted from most of the fun childhood activities that I had enjoyed up to that point, including riding my bicycle, climbing trees, roller skating, swimming, and riding amusement park rides at Busch Gardens or local fairs. I was even restricted from taking physical education (PE) at school with my friends. I had to stay alone in the classroom and work on schoolwork while everyone else enjoyed the warm Florida sunshine. Why was I being punished?

Although I was restricted from the enjoyable activities, did I listen? No! I felt I knew my limits and participated in some activities on a smaller scale and with a great deal of forethought. On days when the seizures were out of control, I would use some commonsense and take it easy. As I got older and was driving, I wouldn't drive if I had seizures that day.

I remember staring out the window watching the neighborhood children running and playing together. I couldn't even spend the night with any of my girlfriends for fear of having another seizure. Sometimes, I hated my extremely sheltered life. I truly felt like the black sheep of the family. I didn't seem to fit in anywhere. I was not a happy child to say the least. Much of that unhappiness was due to the many medications I had to take and the rest was due to my parents protecting me from everything I wanted to do.

After that first grand mal my parents became extremely overprotective, with good reason. As a child, I didn't see it that way. My siblings were too young to understand what their big sister was going through. Because I was somewhat mentally challenged, I seemed to fit in with them and their friends much easier than with children of my own age.

Each visit to the neurologist became a major chore. Since doctors only *practice* medicine, I was an experiment to them. Every appointment began with informing the doctor about my petit mals. After each appointment, I had to become accustomed to either more medication or a different medication in my system. The biggest deal with all the medication changes was the unknown. Would the change in medication or dosage work or not? How many times were the doctors going to change my medications? Questions, doubts, and fear were the story of my traumatic life.

The thing I despised most about my doctor visits was the needles, which always hurt. Every appointment included getting my blood drawn so they could check my medication levels. Although it was only one stick, they usually took no fewer than three tubes. I felt like a human pin-cushion!

Not only was the blood-work a major part of my young life, but so were all the electroencephalograms, (EEGs) I endured. My first EEG occurred while I was in the hospital after the first grand mal. After that, they were repeated once a year or more depending on how I was doing seizure-wise. There were times when I had many petit mals with some lasting longer and appearing more intense. After telling the doctor this, he would sometimes request another EEG. The results were always the same. *The EEG appeared normal; however, there was a shadow in the right temporal lobe area.*

"What was this shadow?" we would ask. As usual we would get the same stupid answer, "It was a gray area and probably nothing." Nothing, hell. I was still having petit mals and that was "not normal."

Although not painful, the EEGs were a pain because I had to pick and comb the wax off my head and out of my hair for the following week. Oh sure, EEGs improved over the years, but I never liked them. The last EEG I had, just before my surgery in 2013, included a full-head EEG of 26 electrodes attached to my scalp with wax. This final EEG was unusual. Instead of going in for just a few hours, I was put in the hospital and monitored for a full week so they could see if or when something happened. I wasn't permitted to have blankets covering my feet or legs, even in the cold hospital. This EEG was done this way so I could be taken off my seizure medications in a controlled environment. If I wanted to go to the bathroom or move to the couch or chair

I had to buzz the desk and let someone know so they could move the cameras to monitor me.

When it was time for the wires to come off, I admit that because of improved methods the nurses used, it was much easier. After removing the wires, the technician placed hot, damp towels on my head and massaged it. What an awesome feeling! Then, she combed out almost all of the wax before I washed my hair. So, yes, it was easier and less inconvenient, but that still doesn't mean I liked it.

After that first grand mal in 1968, I took medication three times a day—every day. My mother had to bring my medications to school and give them to me during lunch because school nurses were not commonplace.

Before the grand mal, I had always liked school. I was an average to above average student with good grades. However, once I returned to school after my grand mal, my love for school changed. Because we tried to keep my disability quiet and didn't broadcast it to everyone, no one understood what I was going through, including my teachers. My grades dropped considerably. I no longer liked school because I didn't fit in anymore. I felt like one of Santa's misfit toys. When groups were picked for different activities, I was always nearly last to be chosen. If that doesn't make a child feel lousy, I don't know what does. I always felt like the odd child out wherever I went and, slowly, I became a loner.

Knowing what I know now about special education, I know in my heart that today I would have been in a class for children with special needs. In the 1960s, though, there were no such classes. The only extra help I received was at home.

Learning became very difficult for me, especially in the areas of reading comprehension and math, because my rate of processing information had been greatly affected by the grand mal. My parents sacrificed countless hours to help me with difficult subject areas. Somehow, I managed to make it through school. My mom always bought books for me to read and my dad helped me with math. My elementary school teachers even told my mom that I was not the same happy, eager child they knew before the grand mal. I had become withdrawn, quiet, and depressed.

Once I entered Kathleen Junior High School, a few things changed. I was still very much a loner and school subjects became even harder. I knew that because I was on so many medications I didn't dare try experimenting with alcohol. I was never interested in smoking because my parents smoked and I hated it! Due to my seizures, I didn't fit in with the smart kids because I couldn't keep up. And, I definitely didn't fit in with the popular group. Was there a group of peers I could ever fit in? School became more and more difficult for me.

The seizures continued to come and go. I was stuck with them and had to learn to live my life around them. In band, I learned to play the clarinet, which came fairly easy since I had a musical background from playing the piano. Some of the "band kids" were the only friends I felt I had. Although I could play the clarinet, I had great difficulty with the written tests, which my band director loved to give, so my grades in band were always quite low. Sadly, I no longer remember how to play either the piano or the clarinet, due to more grand mal seizures over the years.

Due to my parent's income and the fact that they owned a grocery store, social security benefits for my disability wasn't even a thought. Disability was never mentioned to my parents, but my mom did take me to the Epilepsy Foundation in Lakeland once. We left there quite discouraged because all they wanted was donations. No one offered assistance to help pay for any of my expensive medications, which only lasted for a month or so at a time. It depended upon when the doctor changed the prescriptions since my seizures continued. My family always gave and never sought a handout. One year, my dad took me to a turkey shoot where I shot a gun for the first time in my life. I won a turkey, which I donated to a less fortunate family.

My parents had many financial struggles over the years. Somehow, though, we managed to repay each and every medical bill I incurred. Because of my seizure disorder, health insurance wasn't an option since it was considered a pre-existing condition. From the age of nine and a half until I began my teaching career at age 25, every bill had to be paid out-of-pocket by my parents. They had many financial burdens over the years, especially with the store, my medical and pharmaceutical bills didn't help. I always felt it was my fault that we were in debt. I guess it was a good thing that I was restricted from most physical activities; otherwise we may have had many more medical bills.

Chapter 4 ಏ My Dreaded Teen Years

Because nothing up to this point in my life seemed to be any different in regards to the seizures, I continued blaming God for allowing this to happen to me. "Why Me?" was all I could ask. There were so many bad people that deserved this more than I did. But, God's mind was made up. It was my burden, my cross to carry through life. However, I was determined to make the best of an awful situation and that is why I write this today.

As I entered my pre-teen years, I suddenly realized what I was actually going through on a daily basis. I took it upon myself to obtain some medical books from the library and researched my seizures. Once I understood more about my medical condition, I then moved on to learning how to use a Physician's Desk Reference (PDR). I was curious to learn about the drugs that the doctors prescribed and what they should have been doing to stop the seizures. I knew deep down inside that I had to continue to educate myself about my situation so I could explain things to the doctors when they asked questions. By asking questions about my condition, I would be able to understand the doctor's answers.

As the dreaded teenage years progressed, and still nothing had changed in my life seizure-wise, I became increasingly distressed. There were days when I would have so many seizures that I would be totally exhausted by the time I got home from school. They continued to come and go as they pleased and schoolwork became more difficult because I was unable to focus.

Mom and I began to have many issues with one another, fighting constantly. I truly felt that I was treated as the odd child. Every Saturday, I was expected to clean the house, fold towels, scrub the bathrooms, run the sweeper and watch my brothers and sister, and if I was needed to work at the store, then I went with dad for the day. I truly enjoyed working at the store, but I was still expected to do my chores at home and keep up with school. I had a lot of pressure as a child with special needs. As a retired teacher of children with special needs and knowing what should have been done and the help I should have received, I sit and look back on my life as a kid and wonder how in the world I ever did it.

There were times, it seemed to me, as though I was my parents "demon child." My personality had drastically changed from being a sweet, kind little girl to hateful and mean. I always felt that my parents were embarrassed that I was their child, although they never showed it. Due to all my anger problems and fights with my mom, I was sent to a psychiatrist for counseling. At one point during high school, I was on 27 pills a day, yet I still had seizures. Who the hell wouldn't be a head case being on so many medications and treated as an outcast? In retrospect, I feel like that entire period of my life was a joke, as the psychiatrist was absolutely no help. Now when I look back on my teen years and all I went through, I didn't feel like I was being helped at all. I felt as though the doctors only wanted to dope me up with medications that never worked. And they did just that.

My family and I continued to attend the prayer novenas at church with hopes that one day I would be cured of my horrible affliction. I continued asking God, "Why Me?" Although I've never gotten my answer, I am sure that somewhere throughout my life there was or will be a reason for my suffering.

As time went on, the doctors informed us that the Dilantin® they were using to treat the seizures would eventually cause my gums to grow over my teeth. Once they got to where they were getting out of control we would have to have them surgically scraped. This was a very painful procedure. The periodontist did the top gums first and the bottom ones about two weeks later. For me, the worst part of it all was the injections into the gums to numb it before the scraping process began.

At the age of 14, I began thinking about learning to drive. About the same time, my doctor mentioned that I may possibly be able to go off all my medications. Well it sounded like a great idea, but because the doctors couldn't guarantee that nothing would happen while I was driving, my parents answered that idea with a resounding "No!" Instead, the doctors decided that since I had been seizure-free for a year, I could drive as long as I stayed on my medications.

Of course, our definitions of seizure-free didn't quite match. From everything I had learned and read about seizures, I knew what was really happening. That is when I realized that the "dizzy spells", as I called them, were actually petit mal seizures. At the age of 15 I got my restricted driver's license and only drove when necessary.

Then, at 16, when I wanted to take my siblings to Disney World, I was allowed to drive them because I had proven to my parents that I was a responsible driver. I had shown that when I felt a petit mal coming on, I would pull off the road and stop the car. Sometimes, I continued driving and then had no idea where I was when I regained awareness. This was the scariest part of driving, especially when I was alone.

With each and every trip to the doctor, they asked how I felt when a seizure was coming on. That's difficult to answer because the seizures were somewhat unexplainable. The doctors acted as though I didn't know what I was talking about. I do know that it always seemed to begin in my stomach and most of the time I could continue a conversation with someone but never remember any of it. Even if I knew one was coming on, there was nothing I could do about it. There was no stopping the petit mal seizures. I just had to deal with them as a part of my life. Even today, it's difficult to explain to people, doctors included, who have never had a seizure.

Driving appeared to be the least of my worries. Dating age and going out with friends was knocking at my door, so keeping my seizures hidden from those I dated was more challenging than driving. My high school boyfriend knew about my seizures and was very understanding. He began to recognize when I was having one and would just take my hand or hold me close. There were times when I had upwards of 50 petit mal seizures in any given day. The seizures were somewhat controlled with all my medications, still they could and would come at any time. Some days were much worse than others. Because of all the petit mals, I would become extremely tired and just want to sleep.

I was able to hide my seizures from most people until my mom started to figure out when I was having one. I would smack my lips together and stare off into space. I could still carry on a conversation, but it was as if I was in another world and sometimes I would say things that didn't fit into

38

the conversation. Mom started noticing those little things; other people just chalked it up to me not paying attention. Because of my seizures, I could not keep up with lecture classes which caused me to fall behind. Most of my teachers never knew the daily hell I went through and I never received extra help at school.

During a seizure, I could never remember what my conversations were about. That became quite frustrating. At one point I began to run and throw water in my face with hopes that it would help stop the seizure, not a chance! I even tried hitting myself in the head hoping to stop it which didn't work either. At school, I would just put my head down on my desk until it passed.

When I was working at our grocery store, I would get someone to take over, leave the register and run to the bathroom for water. Although this never helped with the seizures, it helped me deal with the situation.

Throughout high school and college, I dreaded any type of group activity. I didn't feel as smart as the other students and I didn't want to speak in front of a group or class for fear of a seizure coming on. I had a hard time finding the right words and forgot the subject. Worst of all, I couldn't take adequate notes. I was still afraid people would find out about my seizures.

As I coped with everyday life through my high school years, I became more and more determined to walk across that stage and receive my diploma at graduation just like everyone else. I was determined to attend college and nothing was going to stand in my way; not even a stupid seizure disorder. I had to graduate high school with at least a C average. Even with all the seizures and the difficulty I had learning, I continued to move forward with my life.

Chapter 5 ∾ Understanding College Life Living with Seizures

I graduated with my class from Kathleen High School in June of 1977 and I started college that fall. I commuted to Polk Community College (PCC) in Winter Haven every day. I was not backing down from my dream of becoming a nurse.

College was a very bumpy road with occasional potholes. By the time I finished most of my basic classes and began the nursing program, I had taken most classes twice. Yes, twice. Some classes, I even took a third time. I had a difficult time retaining the learned material long enough to pass a test on it. Sometimes, I would go so far in a class, drop it, and then retake it. Finally, I decided nursing wasn't for me and majored in special education. I had completed almost all of my basic classes, so I applied to, and amazingly, was accepted at the University of South Florida (USF) in 1980.

Changing my major from nursing to education was not problematic because it occurred during my basic college courses. The nursing program I started at PCC helped me in medical knowledge and it gave me the chance to learn more about my disability.

While at USF, I took the last few classes I needed to earn my Associate of Arts degree. Then, I began my work in the College of Education. Two years later, I received my Bachelor of Arts in Special Education and regular Elementary Education. Due to the difficulty I had with classes, it took me three years at PCC and three years at USF, for a total of six years, to earn my Bachelor's degree. I spent a great deal of time getting extra help from my professors so I could graduate to be a teacher.

Going to a major university like USF was exciting! I started out driving back and forth to Tampa. One day I spotted a campground on my way to school and a wild and crazy idea popped into my head. After class, I inquired about renting a space so I could be closer to college. My parents owned a small travel trailer and I thought it would be just perfect for what I wanted to do. The campground was not too far from USF and I would be on my own. I wanted to do this to get away from the constant questions of "Did you take your medication?" or "Do you feel alright?" Hearing my concerned parents every morning and every night had become quite annoying. I wanted to prove to them and to myself that I could live on my own. Living between home and college would allow me to go home on the weekends and work at the store, do laundry, or sit around the pool at the campgrounds if I preferred. My parents agreed to let me live at the campground and we prepared for my big move. As we were setting up the camper, another young girl and her family pulled in beside us. She was going to do the same thing. How neat was that? I guess great minds think alike!

Everything started out fantastic. I went home on the weekends and did my laundry, bought groceries, and worked at the store when I could. My dad always fixed me up with meat from the meat department so I could cook good meals for myself.

Then one evening my life turned upside down in a matter of minutes. I was in my bed in the camper and started to have a petit mal. Like always I jumped up and went to get water to throw in my face. Then I proceeded to go into the second grand mal of my life, nearly eleven years after the first one!

I fell to the floor and began shaking uncontrollably. As with the first grand mal, I shook and lost control of my muscles. I uncontrollably bit my bottom lip and tongue until they were terribly bruised and bloodied. Throughout the whole ordeal, I didn't lose total consciousness, as I realized there was a space heater on the floor right in front of my face. I knew I couldn't get close to it so I fought with the seizure as it ran its ugly self through my trembling body. Once I regained total consciousness and was able to function, I knew I had to get help because I was in a weakened state. It was late at night, so I went next door and pounded on the door until I woke the girl who lived there.

When she finally answered the door she couldn't believe her eyes. "What happened to you?" she asked. I told her what had just taken place and asked her to walk down to the pay phone with me so I could call my mom and dad. When we got to the phone booth I made that horrifying call home. Upset and scared my mom said, "Dad is on his way." Dad came to get me and said, "Just leave everything as it is. We'll come back for it later."

The following morning, we went straight to the neurologist. The doctor informed us that I would have to wait a year before I could drive again. All I could think was, "Oh, my God, you must be kidding."

As devastating as that was, I was extremely lucky to have parents willing to drive me back and forth to Tampa for classes. We returned to the campgrounds, brought the camper back home and my family became my personal taxi service. They drove me to college, sat in the car waiting for me to get out of class, and drove me home. Talk about dedication, God sure put a lot on their plates.

More than anything, I wanted to complete college and nothing was going to stand in my way. "Would my seizures ever stop? Would they always be in my life?" These were the thoughts that kept going through my mind. After the driving restriction ended, I continued to live at home and resumed the fearful 35 mile drive to college alone.

During my time back home, I began to see a chiropractor for my back issues. He was a great back-cracker and helped. However, he seemed to overstep his bounds, although I didn't realize it at the time. He told me I didn't need my medications, and that he could fix my seizure problems. Because I was at the end of my rope in dealing with my prescriptions and fed up with the fact that God wasn't going to cure me, I put my faith in the chiropractor. "Boy, did I screw up!"

I began to slowly wean myself off of my medications without my neurologist's knowledge and continued to see the chiropractor for back, neck, and head treatments. I soon realized that this was not the smartest decision I'd ever made.

In the spring of 1982, my family installed a swimming pool at our house. We all pitched in and helped to dig the area where the pool would eventually go. I apparently overdid it during the first day of digging. Whether it was due to not taking all my medications or digging being too strenuous for me, it triggered something.

That evening, as my sister De and I were in the bathroom getting ready for bed, I had my third grand mal. Luckily, my mom came in and realized what was happening. As I fell, she caught me and we both went down. All I really remember was coming back to reality and hearing the paramedic tell my parents that I wouldn't be able to drive a car for a year. "Oh, my gosh. Will this ever end?" I wondered.

I had only been driving for a few months since my year of no driving from the second grand mal. Now, once again, Mom and Dad stepped in and become my taxi drivers. This was too much, but I was not giving up on college.

Much time was spent trying to figure out what could be causing my daily petit mal seizures and now the grand mal seizures. Could it be the chocolate I ate so much of or all the stress in my daily life? We even tried to connect it to my menstrual cycle. Nothing appeared to be the culprit, as the seizures just did as they pleased. "Darn" all I wanted to know was, "why can't they just go away?" The third grand mal added more stress because I never knew when another attack would occur. With each petit mal, I worried about how far it would go— "Would it become a grand mal?"

As my second year of no driving was coming to a close, I became anxious to drive, so one morning on the way to USF, I begged my mom to let me. I had been doing better, even though the petit mal seizures continued to interrupt my life at their chosen times. I really didn't think it would be a problem. How wrong I was!

As we headed down Gibsonia-Galloway Road I could feel a petit mal beginning to surface. My mom caught on to what was happening and grabbed the steering wheel. Together, we stopped the car and changed places. "Oh, my God, this has got to end!" I thought. I just wanted to live a normal life, but I was beginning to realize that was impossible.

I continued to press on in college and requested schools close by the college for my student teaching assignments. I didn't want to drive very far with my condition, especially since I had just started driving again. Thank goodness my professors were understanding and kept me close to the college.

Finally, I graduated from USF in June of 1983. I was so proud of myself for completing college and earning my degree. Even though it was a rough ride, I did it! The theme of my graduation party was, *I Did It My Way*, one of my favorite songs by the late Elvis Presley. The song fit my situation perfectly as I had done things my way. It may have been unusual, but I had to adjust my life style to fit my medical issues, so I did it my way!

Chapter 6 ∞   Beginning My Career

When it was time to begin my teaching career, I had many decisions to make regarding my condition. First of all, do I tell the county or principals about my seizures? Hell, no. That would only keep them from hiring me. I knew I could be a great teacher with or without seizures. My sixth interview was at Winston Elementary. Mr. Thompkins was a rather tall, large black man with a humorous personality. He appeared to be quite impressed with me and wanted me to meet his assistant, Mr. Watrous, later that afternoon. Since that was convenient, I decided to grab lunch and return for the meeting. I wanted the job so badly that I told them that I would sit in the waiting room until they hired me. Persistence paid off, I got my first teaching job. How exciting! No one knew about my seizures.

My first year of teaching was about to begin under the direction of "Mr. T" at the rather small, old "Strawberry School". Strawberry schools were prominent in the area from 1928 -1954. Since many families could not afford to hire extra pickers to harvest the strawberries, the children would help. Instead of summer vacation, the children took the winter months off to help with the harvest.

The entire staff at the school was amazing and I met many interesting people and wonderful children. Unfortunately, I continued to deal with seizures. I chose to inform a few of the teachers I became close to just so someone knew my situation. My first grade class met in one of five portables behind the school. It was an incredible year and I enjoyed every minute of it! However, as a teacher with an Exceptional Student Education (ESE) background, I noticed that our school sent our special ed. children to another school because we didn't have an ESE unit.

After I had proven myself that first year, I spoke to Mr. T about starting up a much needed ESE unit, since that was my background. I began creating the unit for the following year. A lot of time, hard work and, of course, my own money went into this new program.

I taught the ESE unit at Winston Elementary for five years before asking to return to first grade where I remained for the next five years. Everything went great during those eleven years of teaching, except that I continued my battle with petit mal seizures.

In 1986, I decided to spread my wings and move into my own place. I wanted to purchase something in my price range. I found a duplex on the south side of town, perfect for one or two people. I applied for the loan and purchased my first home, a duplex. I was able to watch the construction since it was in a newer area. Mr.Watrous, my assistant principal at Winston, gave me a dachshund puppy before I moved in so I would have a companion. Pebbles and I lived with my parents until my duplex was finished. In June of 1987, I made the big move; I was finally going to be on my own. Despite some reservations because of my petit mals, I decided to prove to all of us that I was able to take care of myself.

In January of 1988, while doing wash at my mom and dad's house, I met my future husband, Tracey, a good friend of my brother, Tim. We dated for a short while and soon realized that we were meant to be together. This bothered some family members because Tracey is nine years younger than me. Since age didn't matter to either of us, we moved on. He was aware of my seizures and it was not a hindrance to him. He eventually learned to recognize when I was out of sorts and experiencing a seizure. After experiencing my petit mals, we decided that he would move in with me to help, if needed. He learned about my condition and knew what to discuss with my doctors. We had a large church wedding and beautiful reception in 1989. We spent part of our honeymoon at Daytona Beach and the rest at the happiest place on Earth, Disney World.

Like any couple, we had ups and downs in our marriage. Thank goodness, Tracey has been exceptionally understanding of my seizures, even though they always seemed to get in the way. For example, imagine having a seizure during lovemaking. It never failed. Obviously, this was very difficult for the both of us. However, we were adults and discovered ways to beat this situation.

From the time we met, Tracey shared my seizure nightmare. Most evenings, he came home to find me sleeping after a full day of teaching despite ongoing seizures, and cooked dinner. I could also be extremely moody, which kept our relationship on a roller-coaster ride, so to speak. Tracey became quite protective because of my condition. He even installed a GPS system on my cell phone in case I couldn't find my way home. Most women would look at it as controlling, but I knew my situation and appreciated the fact that Tracey cared so much. Whenever he worked out of town, he'd let our neighbors know that I would be alone. He also called frequently to check on me. Although annoying at times, it was for my own good.

We worked together through the rough times and enjoyed all the good times. After three years of marriage, we planned on trying to have a baby. However, I was blessed with yet another medical issue, endometriosis. Therefore, we weren't sure if I could get pregnant. The endometriosis was so bad that my gynecologist sent me to see a specialist in Tampa who placed me on birth control in hopes of reversing the condition.

After about a year, I went off the birth control medication and much to our amazement, it happened! I was pregnant! I stopped one of my seizure medications to avoid birth defects. Fortunately, I was able to function, even though I continued to have petit mals. My pregnancy was wonderful and I had never felt better. In July 1993, we became the proud parents of a beautiful baby girl, Shayla. Although the pregnancy was awesome, the delivery was another issue. Because my dilation stopped, the hospital sent me home because they thought I wasn't ready to deliver. We returned a couple of hours later when the contractions became unbearable. Dr. Ellington broke my water and gave me pitocin to speed delivery. Leaving the room, he instructed the nurses to continue to monitor Shayla's heart rate.

Eventually, Shayla decided it was time to greet the world. Every time she attempted to enter the world, her head hit the umbilical cord causing her heart rate to drop.

Dr. Ellington wasn't happy when he returned. He held Shayla inside long enough for them to prep for emergency surgery because she was in distress. I had prayed for a C-Section because I felt the stress of normal childbirth might cause me to have another seizure. Either way, I was going to do this. Tracey dressed in his scrubs and with video camera in hand, off we went. Being awake and aware during the birth was the greatest thing ever! Because Shayla had ingested meconium (the first fecal excretion of a newborn), she was immediately placed in the NICU (Neonatal Intensive Care Unit). Because of the C-section, I only caught a quick glance of her as the nurse rushed past me. This was difficult, especially for a first-time mom. Finally, we did get to see our little fighter. After four days they brought her to my room. When we were both stable enough, we were released. However, the doctors didn't want us to take her into public for six to eight weeks because of her weakened lungs.

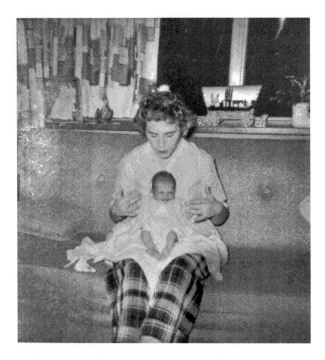

3. Deborah at One Month and Her Mother

In August 1995, I accepted a position at another school beginning a new type of ESE program, ESE inclusion. Three of us made up the "inclusion team." We were placed in a portable along with paraprofessionals and traveled to different regular classrooms providing encouragement and assistance to our students. I taught second, then first grade the following two years, respectively, as inclusion was not my cup of tea. The principal was quite helpful and a joy to be around. I was on a committee that planned and built the float for the Lakeland Christmas Parade. Even with a cast past his knee, Tracey sacrificed countless hours cutting out the wood to make a sleigh and wiring the stereo so we could amplify Christmas music.

Although my first year at Griffin was an enjoyable experience, things didn't go as well during my second and third year. The principal's attitude changed toward me when I went into the classroom instead of inclusion. She seemed to have it in for certain people and made teaching hell. She didn't want to walk into your classroom and find you sitting. She pushed it further when she started to require teachers to wear hosiery. I never felt as though I could do enough to please her. She found fault with everything I did, making me wonder if leaving Winston Elementary had been a huge mistake. The stress at this new job increased my petit mals.

Additionally, while teaching first grade in 1997, Shayla and I were involved in a severe car wreck on South Florida Avenue in Lakeland. I was hit from behind (I was not at fault) and suffered a bad concussion. I missed about a week of school.

When the school year ended, I decided to move to a school closer to our home to reduce our chances of automobile accidents and to return to the ESE classroom. I knew I couldn't continue working in such a stressful environment.

In the fall of 1998, I moved to Lakeland Highlands Middle School. My new assignment was teaching an Educable Mentally Handicapped (EMH) group of students. What an awesome adventure! The principal and his assistant were an awesome pair and the office staff was fantastic.

I was placed in a portable behind the PE area. The students were wonderful and together we experienced many learning accomplishments. Later, I moved into the building for the same class, but most of my teaching was community-based hands-on. Community-based learning meant lots of wonderful field trips so the students would learn real-world life and survival skills outside of the classroom. We went to grocery stores where they learned to compare prices using ads. At restaurants, they learned how to behave, order, and pay. We enjoyed fun activities like miniature golf, bowling, and fishing. My students also cooked many delicious meals and desserts in our classroom and learned many life skills.

During the spring of the 1999, I became ill and was prescribed the antibiotic, Biaxin®. I began taking it over the weekend and by Monday felt that something wasn't quite right. I felt dizzy and confused while I was getting ready for work. Although I drove to work, I didn't remember how I got there. Soon after, my paraprofessional and students entered the class. By then, I was feeling much worse.

Thankfully, my paraprofessional had enough sense to have one of the larger students walk me to the office down the hall. By the time we got there, I was almost completely unconscious. Fortunately, the nurse knew about my situation and immediately called my husband. He directed her to call an ambulance and met me at the hospital. An hour later, my blood work revealed that the mixture of my seizure medications and the antibiotic were incompatible. The ER doctor actually told me that it was a good thing I didn't take any more of the antibiotics as I probably wouldn't have made it to

60

the hospital. After four hours, I was stable enough to be released with a different antibiotic.

Along with teaching and scheduling the community-based learning field trips, I had a great deal of required paperwork for my special needs students. Around this time, my district moved to computer-based forms and I had to learn computer lingo. I discovered that the screen refresh rate increased my daily seizures, which continued throughout the remainder of my teaching career. I realized that as long as I stayed in ESE, computer-based Individual Education Plans (IEPs) would be required. With my sensitivity, this wasn't going to be easy.

By this time, I had recruited my father, who had sold the grocery store and retired, to become a para-specific in my classroom. He worked with only one autistic child and helped him learn patience and coping mechanisms. My father frequently helped me before and after school by scheduling field trips.

The following year, the class moved to the former home economics classroom featuring three kitchens. Between my paraprofessional, my dad, and me, we were able to divide up the class to utilize the kitchens. Our first class project was to make cookies from scratch. Teaching meal preparation in the kitchens was a big improvement over a regular classroom. We also had a washer and dryer in our room, so I was able to teach the students how to separate, wash, and dry clothes. We had so much fun at the beginning of the year.

Then, in October, I was offered a position at another school. It was going to be hard to leave since this was my seventh year at the middle school and the students had really become a major part of my life. But, sometimes we have to do what we have to do.

At my new job site, Bill Duncan Opportunity School, I worked with students in an ESE Expulsion unit, which meant I was dealing with students who had brought drugs, guns, or knives to their home schools or who had thrown furniture at their teachers. I fell in love with the job, the kids, and my colleagues. This was the most rewarding and memorable experience I had throughout my entire teaching career. What was supposed to be a teaching challenge was instead a great success. I loved this job.

During the spring of 2003, my daughter and I both caught a terrible case of the flu. We slept together in the master bedroom closed off from the rest of the house. My husband was able to easily keep an eye on us. One afternoon, I woke up from a nap and reached over to feel Shayla's forehead. She was burning up! I screamed for my husband and he rushed in to see what was wrong. He immediately ran for the Tylenol® and, not thinking, I got out of bed to try to help. This was the wrong action to take because I was already weak and had also been running a fever.

I began to have a grand mal seizure in the middle of the living room. "Really, again?" This was now the fourth grand mal of my life, though it wasn't as serious as the previous ones. I had been doing better until then. Since I could still function to some degree, I told my husband "I'll be fine. Since it was just because of the fever, I shouldn't need to see the doctor just now". I called and told the nurse what had happened and why. She scheduled an appointment with the doctor the next morning.

After two years at Bill Duncan, the county decided to privatize the school. All teachers had to find new schools. I accepted a fourth grade teaching position at Polk City Elementary. The school was about forty miles from home, but choices were slim.

After my first year at Polk City Elementary, the principal who'd hired me retired. During the new principal's first year, I continued teaching fourth grade. In 2006, the new principal informed me that I needed to take the ESE Certification Test to return to the ESE classroom. Was this some kind of sick joke? I had passed my teaching exams and my certificate was still in compliance with the state. I was told I had been out of the regular education classroom for too many consecutive years. Because this principal was going to place me back into an ESE classroom, I had to take the test.

All of this had to do with the 2001, *No Child Left Behind Act* (NCLB). Returning to ESE was not something I really wanted to do at the time, but the principal insisted. Now if this wasn't a stressful situation, I don't know what was. Since I was happy teaching fourth grade because of fewer computer refresh rate-related issues, I decided to explore other options.

The test I was expected to take was a three-hour computer-based test. Immediately, my stress level went through the roof because this seemed impossible. I attempted to take it, but the flickering caused petit mals and caused me to doze. I lost valuable time adversely affecting my score. Depressingly, I did not pass. I was going to have to attempt it again to continue teaching. This situation was driving me crazy and increasing my frequency of seizures.

Because the computer caused more seizures due to the refresh rate and the screen flickering, I fought very hard for a written test. And just to clarify, it wasn't only the computer that I had issues with. I also wasn't able to play on my Nintendo DS® or my computer tablet. Electronic devices just aren't seizure friendly.

I contacted the state and explained my reason for jumping through numerous hoops to get approval for a written test. I was extremely frustrated, and sometimes became quite nasty, while struggling to resolve this situation over the phone.

The stress of getting a letter from the doctor and dealing with the county alone was enough to send me over the edge. I hung in there and fought for my paper and pencil test and extra time that would be necessary. After months of waiting and receiving a letter from my neurologist, the state finally saw the light and allowed me to take a written test. As a special education teacher, I knew these accommodations could be made for me. We, as teachers, did it all the time for students so why was the state being so damn hardheaded with my situation?

The following year, I left Polk City Elementary to teach fourth grade at Scott Lake Elementary, which was much closer to our home. Because I was continuing to retake the test the state wanted, I was hirable. Because of the *NCLB Act*, I had to take the test to continue teaching. None of the other teachers I talked to had heard of such a thing.

I was sure the stress of having to take the test caused my seizures to increase. After failing twice, I had to reapply to take the paper and pencil test. I continued to stand up for myself. I went through this ridiculousness five times before I gave up on it. I decided since I hadn't passed the test, I would take the test for teaching pre-kindergarten through third grade. It was almost three years from the time I took my first test to the time I took the final test. I took it and failed by one point. "What the hell?" It would narrow what I could teach but at that point I wasn't concerned. I would gladly teach pre-kindergarten to third grade.

The entire testing situation was nonsense and then to fight to take it paper and pencil caused so much undue stress that I was ready to walk away from a career that I truly loved. "Why all of this hassle? What had I done to deserve this?" Even today, I still do not understand why I had to take that test. It was such nonsense and no one could give me a straight answer. They just blamed it on the 2001 *NCLB Act.*

I continued to work at Scott Lake for another year. The following year, the only job they would allow me to do was ESE pre-kindergarten. Once again I had to go through the same hassle to take a paper and pencil test. Finally, I passed it and was able to teach ESE pre-kindergarten through third grade. Because Scott Lake didn't have an opening, I was moved to Dixieland to co-teach in an ESE and regular education pre-kindergarten class. This was quite an experience that I enjoyed immensely. Then came the devastating news that they lost the ESE pre-k unit for the following year because there weren't enough ESE students to warrant my job. I was being placed at another school. I accepted the ESE pre-kindergarten unit at Carlton Palmore. At least, it was close to our home. Thank goodness I had such an understanding and helpful husband and daughter. Yet, all this moving from school to school was driving me crazy! All because of the senseless *No Child Left Behind Act*.

I was going to be teaching ESE pre-k and would have a full-time paraprofessional. However, if there was ever a year from Hell, this was it! It turned out to be the most horrible experience of my teaching career, but not because of the children! The principal had no choice but to accept me because I had been displaced. Due to my seniority and the loss of the unit at Dixieland Elementary, I had to be placed somewhere. She wasn't happy about being forced to hire me and showed her true colors. The paraprofessional assigned to my classroom spent very little time helping. She spent more time on her phone, sitting out in her car, or just gossiping with other teachers. I spoke to the principal numerous times regarding this problem but no assistance was offered. It seemed that she was a favorite of the principal and a great way for the boss to set me up so she could get rid of me.

Because the paraprofessional spent so little time in the room with me, I tried to complete IEPs while I was teaching a classroom of 3 and 4 year olds. Once, when I didn't get an IEP totally completed, I was blessed out by our staffing specialist who was a truly evil woman. Due to the refresh rates and blinking screens causing seizures, about 15 minutes was my limit. It was obvious that she ran straight to the principal regarding the IEP being incomplete, because I was quickly reprimanded.

Thus, the principal insisted that I get a note from the doctor regarding my computer time. I was quite upset with this request and didn't understand how she could do this but I complied with her wishes. She made some comments about me not doing my job. The stress at this school, due to the principal and my county contact person was horrendous. There was no excuse for this type of disrespect by either one. It only caused more unneeded stress and eventually other medical issues.

I guess people just don't understand when other people have disabilities. They treat them differently–even to the extent of harassment, which is what I felt was occurring. It seemed obvious that people like that principal don't belong in education in any capacity. They don't care about people and appear to be there only for a paycheck.

During that Year from Hell, 2011 - 2012, I was taken to the clinic because I wasn't feeling well and had asked the school nurse to check my blood pressure. She immediately informed the principal that I needed to see a doctor as my blood pressure was at stroke level. At a walk-in clinic, the doctor placed me on medication until I could see my regular doctor. What else could go wrong, I thought? Geezz, guess I shouldn't have asked that question.

In December of 2011, Tracey, Shayla, and I decided to attend the Trans-Siberian Orchestra concert in Tampa. Since I had never been, I didn't know what to expect. The strobe lights prevented me from enjoying the show. Strobe lights are known to trigger seizures in many epileptics. Even as an adult, the seizures ruined everything for me. I had to sit with my eyes closed and enjoy the music. In October of 2012, Shayla and I, along with a few of her friends, went to Halloween Horror Nights at one of the nearby theme parks. Talk about a waste of money for me! Once again, I had to deal with strobes and flashing lights throughout all of the haunted houses. With my eyes closed most of the time, Shayla and her friends guided me through. I felt like a real burden to her that night. However, I hadn't known what to expect before we went. This was the sheltered life I was forced to live.

Chapter 7 ᴥ   Shattered Dreams

What Did I Do To Deserve This?

I call this chapter *Shattered Dreams* because, after 28 years of dedicating my life to teaching, I was called to the principal's office at Carlton Palmore Elementary on Friday before spring break and the principal informed me that I was basically being charged with child abuse due to accusations made against me. I questioned who made the accusations and was forced to sit and wait while she spoke with someone in the county office about my right to know. I felt this was a basic right. Finally, she showed me a written statement from a paraprofessional who, without permission, had visited my classroom a couple of times because she liked the little ones.

"What the hell was the principal's problem?" I couldn't believe what I was hearing and reading but that's what they were doing. How ridiculous was this? It truly was laughable, as I had never hurt any children in all my years of teaching. I'm sure if I had I wouldn't have lasted as a teacher. I knew that in previous years I was a bit on the sarcastic side and enjoyed joking around with all of my students, not realizing that some of the things I may have said were hurtful and not funny, however it was not abuse!

I immediately contacted my union president at the <u>Polk Education Association</u> (PEA) who told me to say nothing and they would get me an attorney. Meanwhile, the principal was told by the higher-ups in the county office to give me a letter detailing the situation, to take my keys, and to send me home. I realized that this was her way of setting me up to get rid of me. Since I was no longer allowed to be on school property, I couldn't even retrieve my personal items. This really upset me because I had spent thousands of dollars on books and other teaching items for my classes. I was immediately placed on administrative leave with pay while an investigation took place. Eventually everything was determined to be **unfounded.** I had been falsely accused. It was a first year paraprofessional's word against a 27-year veteran teacher with no record of any type of abuse on a child.

No one could ever imagine the pain, suffering, and hurt that I endured. After all I had done to help children such as buying clothes, shoes, food, and school supplies, not to mention hiring a Santa at Christmas time to take gifts to families in need and tutoring without pay. And, for what? To be treated like an abuser!

Because of the accusation against me, my teaching reputation went straight-to-hell in a hurry. It also caused more stress-induced seizures throughout the next few years. Once again, I couldn't understand why God was putting me through all of this nonsense along with the seizures. Talk about putting someone to the test. It didn't make any sense with all the good I had done in my life and the help I had given other people. Nothing I did for children seemed to matter anymore.

After a rather in-depth meeting with county personnel and my union it was decided that for the next two years, I would be placed at another elementary school with a principal who was known for working well with people in my situation. My job entailed less actual teaching and was closer to what paraprofessionals did. However, I never enjoyed a position as much as I enjoyed this one. The children were fabulous and the staff was the greatest! My entire life changed when I was placed at Oscar J. Pope Elementary.

I stayed busy throughout the day and did whatever was asked of me without question. At least I could finish my career in a wonderful, peaceful place. The stress was lifted off my shoulders and things actually began to look positive. I worked in every capacity with students with diverse handicaps for the last two years of my educational career.

Amazingly, I never had any complaints about me. Huh, imagine that! It just goes to show that I was probably right about the previous school's principal. I still suspect that because my 30-year teaching career was coming to an end, they were trying to kick me to the curb to avoid paying my retirement.

As I look back and think of all the wrong that I witnessed, I now realize why God planned things the way he did.

Chapter 8 ಬಿ   Time for Realization

One morning in November of 2012, I went to shower before going to work. When I entered the bathroom, I began to experience another petit mal seizure. Standing and staring into the mirror is all that I actually remember from the incident. My husband later told me what happened. This was now "his" nightmare.

He heard me hit the wall and fall down. He jumped out of the bed and ran into the bathroom to see what happened, and found me on the floor with my head bent forward. Because of the way I had fallen with my head bent down, I wasn't getting sufficient oxygen. Tracey yelled across the house for our daughter, but she didn't hear him. He did a "no-no" by moving me to assure I was able to breathe. By supporting my head and neck, he was able to see that I was barely breathing. He moved me onto a throw rug in the bathroom and ran to get our daughter, Shayla, who stayed with me while he phoned 911. I was still unconscious. Within minutes, an ambulance arrived and there were people everywhere. Barely aware, I had no idea what was happening, although I remember that they kept patting me in the face to awaken me and trying to stop the seizure. I was in the emergency room when I started to gradually come out of my fifth grand mal.

Since I hadn't had a grand mal in a while, I thought I was doing better even though the petit mals continually plagued my existence. It was after that fifth grand mal that I realized this was never going away. Fine, I would deal with it! What the hell, I had dealt with it since I was nine and a half; nearly 45 years of my life. I spent about a week in the hospital and then rested at home. I couldn't drive, per doctor's orders, but this time it was only for six months. I wasn't sure why the timeline had changed from a year to six months, but I would handle it. Oh, no, "But, what about work?" I didn't want to give up, yet. I began to seriously think about retiring. I would have completed 30 years teaching if I could last until June. My health was more important.

I was also losing income because of missing so much work without sufficient sick leave. Our daughter spoke up and said she would help out by driving me back and forth. If she was ever unable to, Tracey's job was flexible, allowing him to go in late or leave early, if necessary. Sometimes, I even had to rely on my mom and dad to pick me up at school if my husband couldn't. That meant the world to me and knowing I could finish my 30 years was such a blessing. My husband and I had discussed retirement but I really didn't want to leave the children. But, what was best for me?

As I neared the end of my career, I happened to watch a movie called *Gifted Hands*. It truly moved me and started me thinking. My husband also caught the documentary about *Dr. Ben Carson, Pediatric Neurosurgeon*, done in addition to the movie. Tracey recorded it and that afternoon he invited me to sit and watch it with him. When it was over we began to discuss the possibility of me having surgery. I seriously couldn't believe that after 45 years of suffering, there may be a normal future for me. This had to be God's way of showing me something positive.

At my next visit with my neurologist, I asked him about the surgery that Dr. Carson had successfully performed and that I would really like to entertain the idea of the surgery. He encouraged me and referred me to an epileptologist in Tampa. Wow, my future was beginning to look up.

Before anything could get started, I had to see a neuropsychologist for a psychological evaluation. Beginning to the end, the test took five hours, not counting the hour for lunch. Lo and behold, she found exactly what I knew all along, I had a processing deficit. This was the main reason for my trouble in school and with daily routines. There were some other weak areas, but hopefully with the surgery, they would disappear in time.

4. 2013 EEG video monitoring

About a week later, I received a call from the Epilepsy Coordinator at Tampa General Hospital. We scheduled a week of EEG video monitoring during my spring break to keep me from missing more work. Although I was in for the monitoring, I felt like I was at a resort. Everyone was wonderful and the staff was so professional!

5. Sunset from Tampa General Hospital

Everything went great. I had a beautiful sunset out my hospital room window, so every night Shayla and I would visit and take photos. Shayla stayed with me during my monitoring at the hospital's request. She would go downstairs where they had a Starbucks and a McDonalds. Yes, that was heavenly! Since I didn't have any diet restrictions, I could have whatever I wanted. The nurse that attached the electrodes in my head had Shayla go home and get everything that I had that would possibly cause a seizure. Shayla returned with my electronic tablet, Nintendo DS®, cell phone, and plenty of chocolate.

The hardest part of the entire stay was remembering to call the desk and let them know when I was moving about the room. They had to move the camera so they would capture all my activity in case of an issue.

At night, Shayla and I Skyped® or played Jenga™. Try playing Jenga™ on a shaky bedside table. It's hard to keep those pieces from falling and waking up other patients. Along with Shayla, my husband and my parents visited several times. It was such a great stay, even for being in the hospital.

My doctors slowly took me off my seizure medications and hoped for seizure activity during the test. I had an alert button to push if I felt any seizure activity start. When the first one occurred and I pushed the button, an alarm sounded, the television shut off, and the overhead light came on. Suddenly, doctors and nurses came from everywhere. Every time I had to push the button this occurred. I had many petit mals, as well as grand mals that week. According to the data, I'd had seventeen grand mals that occurred while I was sleeping. Finally, one doctor was actually able to understand what I was talking about when I tried to explain my petit mal seizures. He said, "It starts like a rising in the stomach."

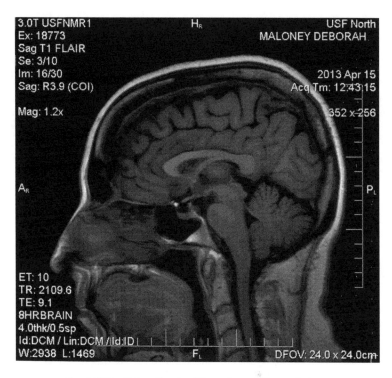

6. MRI of the Brain Showing Affected Area

He hit that nail on the head! "Why didn't any of the other doctors I had seen before know this?" It was time to wait for the next step. Ghee whiz! Two more tests were required in order for me to be a candidate for the surgery.

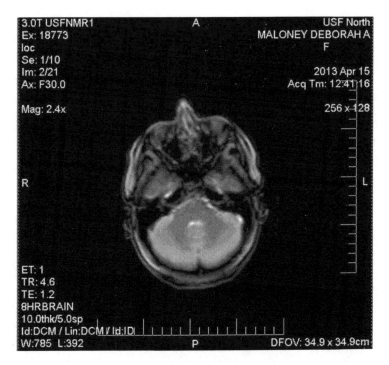

3.0T USFNMR1   A   USF North
Ex: 18773   MALONEY DEBORAH A
loc   F
Se: 1/10
Im: 2/21   2013 Apr 15
Ax: F30.0   Acq Tm: 12:41:16

Mag: 2.4x   256 x 128

R   L

ET: 1
TR: 4.6
TE: 1.2
8HRBRAIN
10.0thk/5.0sp
Id:DCM / Lin:DCM / Id:ID
W:785 L:392   P   DFOV: 34.9 x 34.9cm

7. MRI of Brain Presurgical

First was the <u>positron emission tomography</u> (PET) scan, which shows how organs and tissues are working. Next was a <u>magnetic resonance imaging</u> (MRI), which produced detailed pictures of my brain. These were scheduled on the same day, two weeks after the EEG, to make things easier for me.

When those were complete, the coordinator called me and said the doctors wanted me to have The *Wada* test, also known as the <u>intracarotid sodium amobarbital procedure</u> (ISAP). This was good news because it meant the surgery would probably happen. The *Wada* test determines which side of the brain controls language function and measures memory function of each side of the brain. For the *WADA* test, they put a catheter in through the femoral artery (at the hip) and up to the brain, putting one side of the brain to sleep at a time. I was awake through it all, even though half my brain was asleep at the time. I truly felt like I was in great hands, so I wasn't nervous, highly unusual for me. In fact, it was all quite interesting.

I was able to watch on the computer monitors as the catheter moved from my femoral artery through my body and up to the brain. Excitement was building! Another test down! Now it was time to discuss surgery. I was given a CD-ROM with the pictures of my brain and was able to actually see the section causing all my problems. This was the most amazing thing I had ever seen! The experience alone was worth every bit I went through.

Well, joy! My husband, parents, and I met with the surgeon who would perform my surgery. He informed us that only 10% of the people with seizures like mine can be helped by this particular surgery, and of that 10%, 80% of them could become seizure-free for the rest of their lives. What a day for all of us. Excitement seemed to fill the entire atmosphere knowing all this seizure mess could come to an end and that I could live the rest of my life seizure-free and no longer be fearful of what the next day would bring.

Since nothing in life is guaranteed, the surgery would be a chance I could take or continue my life of unhappiness knowing I didn't try to do something. I was up for the challenge and ready to move on with my life.

My surgery was scheduled for June 24, 2013. The doctor felt assured that all the seizures would stop and, eventually, I would be able to go off my medications. Dr. Carson began doing his first surgeries on the brains of children with seizures in the 1980s. Because of great success with these surgeries, they are currently being done throughout the world. My surgery was originally known as a right temporal lobectomy. It is now known as selective anterior mesial temporal lobe resection of the hippocampus/amygdala.

I feel that I owe so much to the neurologist in Lakeland, Dr. Dillulo, for doing his job of sending me to the right people to get things moving. After all, the surgery was nothing new, about 25 years old, and should have been brought up long before 2013. I also owe so much to Dr. Carson for sharing his life story on television for all to see.

All I ever wanted was to have a normal life without the constant worry of when the next seizure might strike. I had hoped to enjoy my retirement with my husband, travel to places we've never been, and do things I've never done. I hoped and prayed the surgery would go well and the seizures would finally end. If I had to stay on some medications then so be it, but if all worked in my favor and going off the medications was an option then, "Hey, let's do this!"

The Sunday before my surgery, my family and I went to mass. We spoke to one of the priests we had known for years and explained to him that I was having brain surgery on Monday. He immediately stopped what he was doing and anointed my head with oils and prayed with us. Although he didn't know about my seizures, he knew our family. After he anointed me and said some prayers with all of us, I truly felt prepared for the surgery.

88

Chapter 9 ∞ Moving On

On Monday morning, my husband and I were up early and ready to go. We had to be at Tampa General Hospital by 7:00 a.m. Excited about the surgery and the possible changes it could bring to my life, we arrived at the hospital much earlier than necessary. My sister and one of my brothers flew in from Washington D.C. to be with us. My parents were there along with two of my sister's friends. This was a big moment and after everything I had been through, believe me, I was ready.

Everyone said, "See you, later." The nurses whisked me off to the operating room. That was the last thing I remember until I woke up about six hours later. I was awake and alert, but my head was definitely pounding. I remained in the hospital for five days. I was on pain medications, both intravenous (IV) and oral. The pain medications worked, but when they began to wear off my head felt like it was going to explode. The pounding in my head seemed unbearable at times, but I got through it.

I had to be able to eat and drink without any problems as well as use the restroom before I could be released to go home. Once the pain eased up, I was able to get out of the bed and walk the hall. I was ready to go home! The surgery was over and I made it through it!

Finally, I was home in my own bed. The pain returned and the oral medication was nothing compared to the IV medication. With Tracey's help and calming nature, I got through the first week at home. The pain started to ease up and I slowly began to get back to my daily routine in the house. I had to be careful of everything I did, of course, no lifting. During this recovery time, Tracey did his job from home so he could be with me until I was up and around and the pain was pretty well gone.

My surgery was done on June 24th and a week later we were over at Disney's Fort Wilderness Campgrounds for the Independence Day festivities with our neighbors. After sitting out on the grass and enjoying the lovely fireworks display, we stayed the night with them in their RV. This was such an amazing weekend and very relaxing even though I was still on pain medication. The most amazing part of this was that I realized while walking through Fort Wilderness that I could smell things I had never smelled before. The smell of fresh-cut grass, blooming flowers, the sand at the beach area, and even other barbeques were astonishing to me. In that short weekend, I experienced so much that I had missed for all those years. It was like being born as an adult and having skipped my childhood.

My plans were to return to work when school started back in the fall of 2013. I had finished my 30th year of teaching in early June before my surgery, but I wanted to keep working if everything turned out for the best. However, after all I had been through, I wasn't sure if I could go back to work. Heck, I just had brain surgery. Is working possible? During my post-op visit with the surgeon, he released me for work, but cautioned me not to work around children for fear of being hit in the head. Well, working around the children was my job. After much discussion, the decision was made.

When I returned to work in the fall, I worked in the office and helped out some of the teachers setting up their classes. I put up bulletin boards, cut out laminated materials, and helped fill backpacks for students who needed school supplies.

I had decided to retire as of August 27, 2013. That was one of the hardest days of my life because I had to leave my career as a teacher. I didn't want a big party like most people. I just quietly and sadly left the school and walked away. I cried all the way home, but I knew in my heart this was the best decision for me.

I've always believed the saying, "What doesn't kill you will make you stronger!" That little saying sure had a BIG impact on my life. Although there were times that I certainly thought my seizures would kill me, they didn't. They definitely made me a stronger and more determined person. I knew that if I was going to survive, I had to remain strong and determined. Up to this point I had accomplished the goals I set early on in my life, and I did it with a disability.

Since my surgery, I have retired from teaching and I have truly been blessed with a wonderful new life. After my first grand mal at age nine and a half until the surgery, I never realized all that I had missed in life. It is hard to believe that I missed out on so many things that most people take for granted. I've been able to remember things much better than before.

My husband and I enjoy camping with a group. It is incredibly relaxing and enjoyable. I've now been able to drive my retirement gift, a fully loaded black Camaro. I can also ride my bike, provided I wear my helmet. I was unable to drive from November of 2012 until May of 2013, but because I had the surgery in June, my surgeon wanted me to wait the full year before I started driving again. I waited the entire time like a good girl. I began driving again in November of 2013. Since the surgery, I feel like I can come and go as I please without worrying. That is the best part of all of this. I no longer have to worry about when the next seizure is going to disrupt my life.

Nine months after my surgery, everything was going so great that I called my epilepsy coordinator who then contacted the doctor. They decided to slowly wean me off my medications instead of going back in the hospital. Fantastic!!! I am off one medication thus far and have one more to go!

Tapering off the medication is a long and slow process, but in the long run it will be worth it.

I had my annual visit with the surgeon and he is very pleased with my progress. In fact, he has released me except for the medication reduction process. The next step in my reduction will be the true sign, as I will be on less than half of my original medications. The doctor preferred a slow reduction with at least six more months in between. I am fine with that, as everything is going so wonderfully that I don't want to mess it up.

Chapter 10 ໕   A Brand New Me

Since we met with the surgeon, I have taken a second psychological test. Amazingly enough, my new diagnosis was "none." In other words, my disability has been removed. Dr. Henley was greatly impressed with these new results. The day I heard this diagnosis was as exciting to me as the day I had my surgery. I couldn't believe what she was telling me. Now I feel as though I can conquer the world!

Tracey and I, along with our camping group, have been to Gatlinburg, Tennessee, where I was able to experience so many new things for me, including white water rafting. We rented dune buggies and rode up through the mountains. I even got to drive the dune buggy... way too much fun! I had ridden horses as a child, so we enjoyed a horseback riding tour up through the mountains. It was a wonderful time with lots of new adventures. Since our trip, we have also returned to Fort Wilderness for the 4th of July. What an amazing weekend! There just aren't words to describe what a wonderful new life I have.

8. My Independence Day 2013—1 Week Post-Op

I finally got to go out and have a "real drink" with my 21-year old daughter. I never touched alcohol because the results could be devastating with all the medications I took. Now, it is game on! Since March 7, 2015, I have been off all my seizure medications and doing fabulously! I stay in touch with the surgeon, Dr. Vale, from time to time just to keep him in the loop on my status.

I have come to realize that none of this would have been possible without the hand of God guiding me along. Oh sure, my young life was devastating, but I am enjoying every minute of my new life today. The saying, "The Lord works in mysterious

96

ways" is so true. And when He brings you to something He will see you through it, just as He has done with me.

Author

 Deborah Maloney, a retired elementary and special education teacher, lives in Lakeland, Florida, with her husband Tracey. They have been married for more than 25 years. The couple has one adult child and is looking forward to grandchildren someday. She continues to volunteer in the classroom and tutors children after school. Deborah loves working with children and teaching them new and interesting things.

She and Tracey enjoy traveling with their camping group, visiting other cities and states, and seeing the sites this country has to offer. When she is not camping, she enjoys drawing, painting, and scrapbooking.

Throughout her life she struggled immensely with a seizure disorder that caused her to miss out on many things that others take for granted. She is now motivated to educate those with both physical and mental limitations how she overcame her problem. She hopes that by sharing her story, others will see that there is always hope. Going from **Mud Pies and Jump Ropes** to roller coasters and camping has truly been a blessing for her.

Her favorite adage is one that truly hits home with her past.

"When life hands you lemons,

don't just stand there.

Make Lemonade!

Made in the USA
Charleston, SC
30 August 2016